A Slice of CHRISTMAS
from Piece O' Cake Designs

LINDA JENKINS & BECKY GOLDSMITH

C&T PUBLISHING

© 2003, Linda Jenkins and Becky Goldsmith

Editor-in-Chief: Darra Williamson

Editor: Lynn Koolish

Technical Editor: Sara Kate MacFarland

Copyeditor/Proofreader: Linda Smith, Jenni Morrison

Cover Designer: Kristen Yenche

Design Director/Book Designer: Kristen Yenche

Illustrators: Becky Goldsmith and Richard Sheppard

Production Assistants: Lucas Mulks and Kirstie L. McCormick

Quilt Photography: Chris Marona unless otherwise noted

How-to Photography: Diane Pedersen

Published by C&T Publishing, Inc., P.O. Box 1456, Lafayette, California 94549

Front cover: *The Christmas Trees* by Becky Goldsmith

Back cover: *1950s Santa Claus* by Linda Jenkins, *A Sampling of Santas* by Becky Goldsmith

Attention Copy Shops: Please note the following exception—Publisher and author give permission to photocopy pages 11–14, 19–28, 32–33, 39–42, 46, and pullout sheets for personal use only.

Attention Teachers: C&T Publishing, Inc. encourages you to use this book as a text for teaching. Contact us at 800-284-1114 or www.ctpub.com for more information about the C&T Teachers Program.

We take great care to ensure that the information included in this book is accurate and presented in good faith, but no warranty is provided nor results guaranteed. Because we have no control over the choices of materials or procedures used, neither the author nor C&T Publishing, Inc. shall have any liability to any person or entity with respect to any loss or damage caused directly or indirectly by the information contained in this book. For your convenience, we post an up-to-date listing of corrections on our web page (www.ctpub.com). If a correction is not already noted, please contact our customer service department at ctinfo@ctpub.com or at P.O. Box 1456, Lafayette, CA 94549.

Trademarked (™) and Registered Trademark (®) names are used throughout this book. Rather than use the symbols with every occurrence of a trademark and registered trademark name, we are using the names only in the editorial fashion and to the benefit of the owner, with no intention of infringement.

Library of Congress Cataloging-in-Publication Data

Goldsmith, Becky.

A slice of Christmas from Piece O'Cake Designs / Becky Goldsmith and Linda Jenkins.

p. cm.

ISBN 1-57120-198-X

1. Christmas decorations. 2. Patchwork. I. Jenkins, Linda. II. Piece O'Cake Designs. III. Title.

TT900.C4 .G64 2003

745.594'12--dc21

2002151952

Printed in China

10 9 8 7 6 5 4 3 2 1

Table of Contents

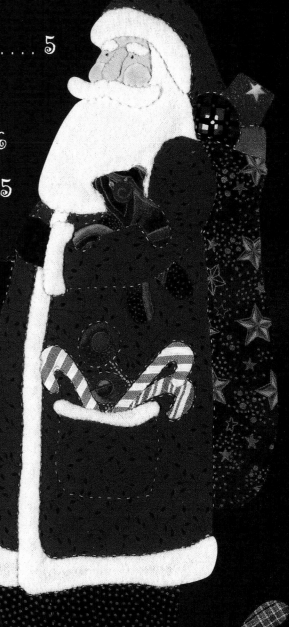

Dedication

Many thanks to all of you who have supported us over the years. It's so rewarding to see the "Piece O' Cake" quilts that you have made. You all keep up the good work!

We thank our husbands, Paul Jenkins and Steve Goldsmith, who are two of the finest men on the planet. Thank you both for your love and support. Please don't ever stop.

Acknowledgments

Many thanks to Lynn Koolish, our editor at C&T. Her expertise is just one of the reasons we are so happy to be working with C&T.

Quilters love fabric and we are no exception. We thank P&B Textiles for supporting us with fabric! They gave us the opportunity to design fabric and we are very grateful for that.

The following companies happily supplied us with batting and felt to use in the projects in this book. A big thank you goes to:

Hobbs Bonded Fibers (Organic Cotton Batting)

Fairfield Processing Corp. (Soft Touch Batting)

Kunin Felt

Introduction

Christmas comes but once a year… and it comes every year! That means it's always a good time to make a Christmas quilt.

We always enjoy making quilts for Christmas. It's a special time of the year. Yes, it's a busy and bustling time, but it's also the time of year that we stop to remember those we love and care about.

Quilts make wonderful gifts. The lucky person who receives a quilt, be it large or small, will never forget who made it—just for them! When you give a quilt to someone, it is like giving away a warm hug that's always handy.

Who doesn't look forward to decorating the house with festive quilts for Christmas? We especially enjoy being reunited with those special holiday quilts that we put away after the holidays last year. Hanging the Santa quilt means that Christmas is near!

We've combined some of our favorite Christmas projects for this book. Some of them come from books and patterns that are now out of print. One of them is brand new. We hope you enjoy finding these old friends again.

Basic Supplies

Fabric: All of the fabrics used in the quilts in this book are 100% cotton unless otherwise noted. We pre-wash our fabric before using it. This is a good way to test for colorfastness. If the fabric is going to shrink, it does so before it is sewn into the quilt. The fabric is easier to work with and smells and feels better if it is pre-washed.

We used polyester felt for the Christmas stockings and tree skirt. We did not pre-wash the felt. If you fuse felt appliqué pieces, test a scrap first. If your iron is too hot, the felt may melt.

Thread: Use cotton thread with cotton fabric. There are many brands to choose from. Work with different brands until you find the one that works best for you.

Batting: We prefer cotton batting. Our favorite is Hobbs Organic Cotton Batting.

Needles for hand appliqué: Linda uses a size 12 John James sharp and Becky uses a size 11 Hemming & Son milliner needle. There are many good needles. Find the one that fits *your* hand.

Pins: Use ½" sequin pins to pin your appliqué pieces in place.

Fusible web: If you prefer to fuse and machine stitch your appliqué, use a paper-backed fusible web. For cotton use a light- or medium-weight fusible. For felt, use a heavy-weight fusible.

Non-stick pressing sheet: If you are doing fusible appliqué, a non-stick pressing sheet will protect your iron and ironing board.

Scissors: Use embroidery-size scissors for both paper and fabric. Small scissors are better for intricate cutting.

Rotary cutter, mat, and acrylic ruler: When trimming blocks to size and cutting borders, rotary cutting tools will give you the best results.

Pencils: Use either a white chalk pencil or a mechanical pencil to draw around templates onto the fabric.

Permanent gel pens: Permanent gel pens come in a variety of colors and are perfect for making the Santa faces.

Permanent markers: To make the positioning overlay, an ultra-fine-point Sharpie marker works best on the upholstery vinyl.

Clear upholstery vinyl: Use 54"-wide clear medium-weight upholstery vinyl to make the positioning overlay. You can usually find it in stores that carry upholstery fabric.

Clear heavy-weight self-laminating sheets: Use these sheets to make templates. You can find them at most office supply stores and sometimes at warehouse markets.

Sandpaper board: When tracing templates onto fabric, place the fabric on the sandpaper side of the board. Then place the template on the fabric. You'll love the way the sandpaper holds the fabric in place when you trace.

Wooden toothpick: Use a round toothpick to help turn the turn-under allowance at points and curves. Wood has a texture that grabs and holds.

Full-spectrum work light: These lamps give off a bright and natural light. A floor lamp is particularly nice as you can position it over your shoulder. Appliqué is so much easier when you can see what you are doing.

Appliqué supplies

1950s Santa Claus Quilt

Made by Linda Jenkins, 2000

Finished appliqué block size: 12" x 12"

Finished Ohio Star block size: 6" x 6"

Finished quilt size: 53" x 66"

Linda used a variety of background fabrics in the blocks to give the quilt more visual texture. She also pieced a special quilt for Santa's bed.

MATERIALS

Brown / tan backgrounds:
A variety of fabrics to total 1⅝ yards

White / brown floors and ground: A variety of fabrics to total ½ yard

Appliqué: A wide variety of fabric scraps

Muslin faces: ⅛ yard

Red and white sashing: ⅝ yard

Green inner border and star centers: ⅜ yard

Checked outer border: 1¾ yards

Red star points: ¼ yard

Striped binding: ¾ yard

Backing and sleeve: 4 yards

Batting: 57" x 70"

Permanent gel pens: A variety of colors to draw the Santa faces

Silk ribbon: A variety of colors to decorate packages

Embroidery floss: A variety of colors

CUTTING

BROWN, WHITE, AND TAN FABRICS
Block backgrounds:

Block #1: Cut 1 square 14" x 14" for the background.

Block #2: Cut 1 rectangle 12¼" x 14" for the background and 1 rectangle 2¼" x 14" for the floor.

Block #3: Cut 1 rectangle 11¾" x 14" for the background and 1 rectangle 2¾" x 14" for the floor.

Block #4: Cut 1 rectangle 8" x 14" for the background and 1 rectangle 6½" x 14" for the floor.

Block #5: Cut 1 square 14" x 14" for the background.

Block #6: Cut 1 rectangle 10¼" x 14" for the background and 1 rectangle 4¼" x 14" for the floor.

Block #7: Cut 1 rectangle 11" x 14" for the background and 1 rectangle 3½" x 14" for the floor.

Block #8: Cut 1 rectangle 11¾" x 14" for the background and 1 rectangle 2¾" x 14" for the ground.

Block #9: Cut 1 rectangle 11½" x 14" for the background and 1 rectangle 3" x 14" for the ground.

Block #10: Cut 1 rectangle 11¾" x 14" for the background and 1 rectangle 2¾" x 14" for the ground.

Block #11: Cut 1 rectangle 12¼" x 14" for the background and 1 rectangle 2¼" x 14" for the ground.

Block #12: Cut 1 rectangle 12½" x 14" for the background and 1 rectangle 2" x 14" for the ground.

RED AND WHITE FABRIC
Sashing: Cut 11 strips 1½" x width of the fabric.
Seam together as needed to cut:

  A. 8 strips 12½" long for short sashing between blocks.

  B. 5 strips 38½" long for sashing between rows.

  C. 2 strips 53½" long for side sashing.

GREEN FABRIC
Inner Border: Cut 5 strips 1" x width of the fabric.
Seam together as needed to cut:

  2 strips 40½" long for top and bottom inner border.

  2 strips 54½" long for side inner border.

Ohio Star centers: Cut 4 squares 3½" x 3½".

CHECKED FABRIC
Outer Border: Cut 2 strips lengthwise 8" x 43" for top and bottom borders and 2 strips lengthwise 8" x 56" for side borders.

Ohio Star block sides: Cut 3 strips 2" x width of the fabric, then cut into 16 squares 2" x 2" for the corners of the blocks and 16 rectangles 2" x 3½".

RED FABRIC
Ohio Star block star points: Cut 2 strips 2" x width of the fabric, then cut into 32 squares 2" x 2" for the star points.

STRIPED FABRIC
Binding: Cut 1 square 25" x 25" to make 2½"-wide continuous bias binding (refer to pages 59-60 for instructions).

BLOCK ASSEMBLY
Santa Blocks

The blocks in the quilt are numbered from left to right, top to bottom. For example, Block #1 is located in the upper left hand corner of the quilt. Full-size appliqué patterns are on a pullout at the back of the book. Because they are placed to fit on the pullout, they are not in numerical order.

1. Sew the ground/floor pieces and the background pieces together as needed.

2. Appliqué the blocks. Refer to pages 49–55 for instructions on making placement overlays and preparing the appliqué.

Appliqué and Embellishment Tips

Use the *cutaway appliqué* technique for Santa's mustache and other small pieces, the *reverse appliqué* technique for the belt buckles, and the *circle appliqué* technique for the snowballs. (Refer to pages 56–58 for instructions.)
A few appliqué pieces (like Santa's beard) will sometimes be divided into two parts, with a different number on each part. For these pieces, stitch down the first part of the piece with the lowest number. Stitch down the next appliqué piece(s) in numerical sequence, then stitch down the second part of the appliqué piece when its number comes up.

For the faces: Tape a piece of muslin over the drawing of each face. The tape keeps the fabric from shifting while you draw. Use permanent gel or paint pens and trace the eyes and fill in the mouth. Santa's beard and mustache cover the edges of his mouth. Look at the quilt on page 6 to see how Linda used her pens.

Santa's Quilt (Block #4)

- Cut 10 strips 1½" x 12" from a variety of fabrics and sew them together. Press all seam allowances in the same direction.

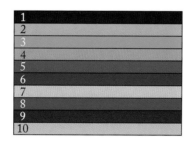

- Cut the pieced strips into 8 strips 1½" wide.

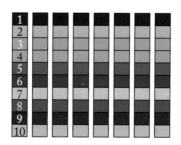

- Turn every other strip upside down and shift the strips as shown. Sew the strips together.

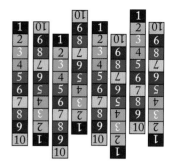

- Place the quilt template (appliqué piece #13) on the diagonal in the center of the unit and trace around it. Cut out the quilt and appliqué in place.

3. After the appliqué and embroidery are complete, press the blocks on the wrong side.

4. Trim the blocks to 12½" x 12½".

BORDER ASSEMBLY
Border Appliqué

Make paper patterns for the borders as follows to ensure correct placement of the border appliqué pieces. Refer to the photograph of the quilt on page 6 for placement. Make sure you keep the appliqué at least ¼" away from the outer edges of the paper, as these are the finished edges of the border.

1. Cut 2 pieces of paper 6" x 41" for the top and bottom borders. With a ruler, draw the center horizontal and vertical lines. Trace the templates for the train onto these pieces of paper. (Full-size border patterns are on pages 11-14.) *Note: Turn the templates upside down to reverse the top train.*

2. Cut 2 pieces of paper 6" x 54" for the side borders. Draw the center lines as in Step 1. Trace the templates for the toys onto the paper.

3. Create placement overlays from the paper patterns.

4. Press each fabric border background in half horizontally and vertically to establish the center lines.

5. Appliqué and embroider the borders. After the appliqué and embroidery are complete, press the borders on the wrong side.

 Appliqué Tips

Use the *reverse appliqué* technique for the train windows, the *circle appliqué* technique for the wheels, and the *cutaway appliqué* technique for the candy canes, propeller, rocking horse, and other small or irregular-shaped pieces. (Refer to pages 56-58 for instructions.)

6. Trim the top and bottom borders to 6½" x 41½". Trim the side borders to 6½" x 54½".

Ohio Star Blocks

 Sewing Tip

For a quick way to sew the star points without marking the diagonal lines, refer to Piecing Triangle Corners on page 59 or use the instructions that follow.

1. Draw a diagonal line on the wrong side of the 2" x 2" star points.

2. Place a 2" x 2" star point over one half of a 2" x 3½" rectangle, right sides together. Sew on the drawn line.

3. Trim the excess ¼" away from the seamline, as shown. Press open.

4. Place a 2" x 2" star point over the other half of the rectangle, right sides together. Sew on the drawn line.

5. Trim the excess ¼" away from the seamline, as shown. Press open.

6. Arrange the pieced units and corner squares. Sew them together into three rows as shown below. Sew the rows together to finish the star. Press the seams in one direction. This block is now 6½" x 6½".

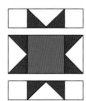

7. Make 3 more Ohio Stars.

QUILT ASSEMBLY

Refer to the Quilt Assembly Diagram on page 10. When sewing the sashings, press the seam allowances toward the sashing after each step. When sewing the borders, press the seam allowances toward the border after each step.

1. Sew the blocks and short sashings (marked A) together into rows.

2. Sew the rows together with the five horizontal sashing strips (marked B).

3. Sew the side sashings (marked C) to the quilt.

4. Sew the top and bottom inner borders to the quilt.

5. Sew the side inner borders to the quilt.

6. Sew the top and bottom outer borders to the quilt.

7. Sew an Ohio Star block to each end of the side outer borders.

8. Sew the side outer borders to the quilt.

9. Add the silk ribbon embellishments. *Do not press the silk ribbon.*

10. Finish the quilt. Refer to pages 55, 60-61 for instructions.

Quilt Assembly Diagram

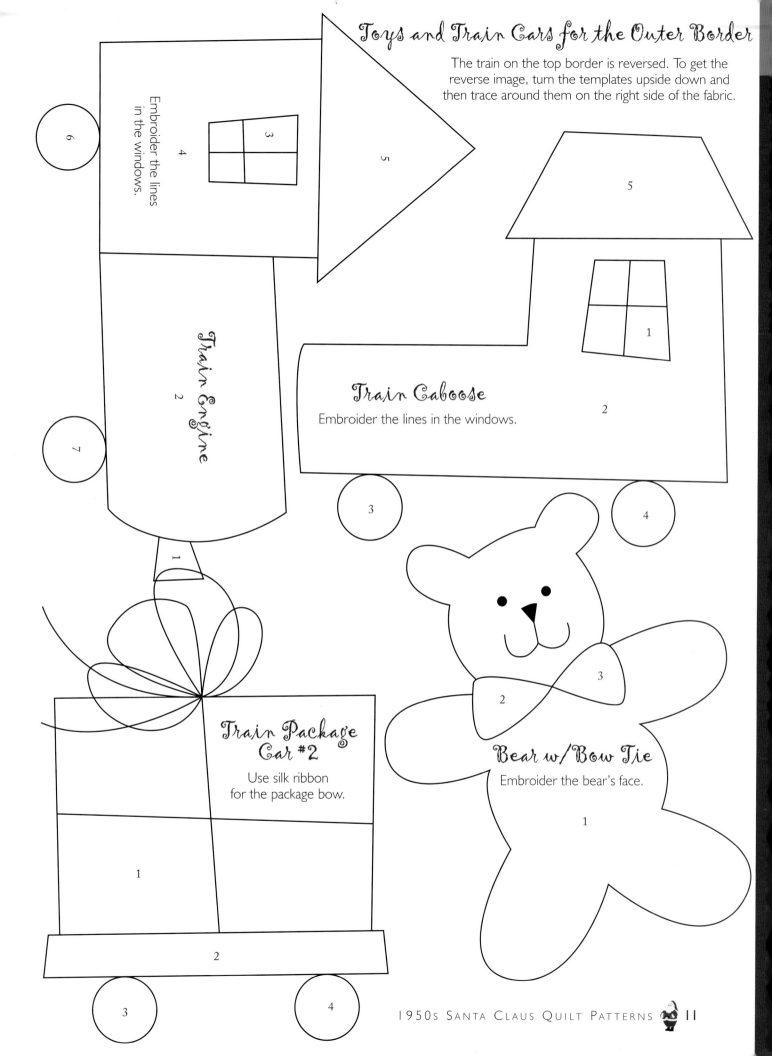

Toys and Train Cars for the Outer Border

The train on the top border is reversed. To get the reverse image, turn the templates upside down and then trace around them on the right side of the fabric.

6

3

4

5

Embroider the lines in the windows.

5

7

Train Engine

2

1

Train Caboose

Embroider the lines in the windows.

2

3

4

1

Train Package Car #2

Use silk ribbon for the package bow.

3

2

Bear w/Bow Tie

Embroider the bear's face.

1

1

2

3

4

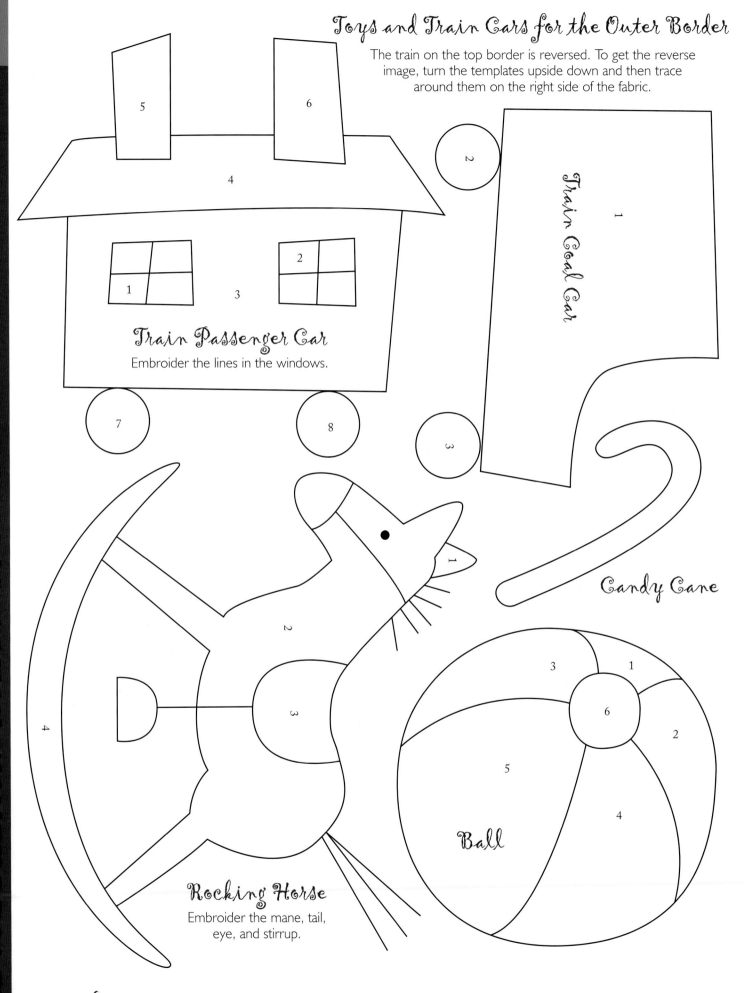

Toys and Train Cars for the Outer Border

The train on the top border is reversed. To get the reverse image, turn the templates upside down and then trace around them on the right side of the fabric.

5

6

4

2

1

Train Coal Car

2

1

3

Train Passenger Car

Embroider the lines in the windows.

7

8

3

Candy Cane

1

2

3

3

1

6

2

4

5

Ball

4

Rocking Horse

Embroider the mane, tail, eye, and stirrup.

Toys for the Outer Border

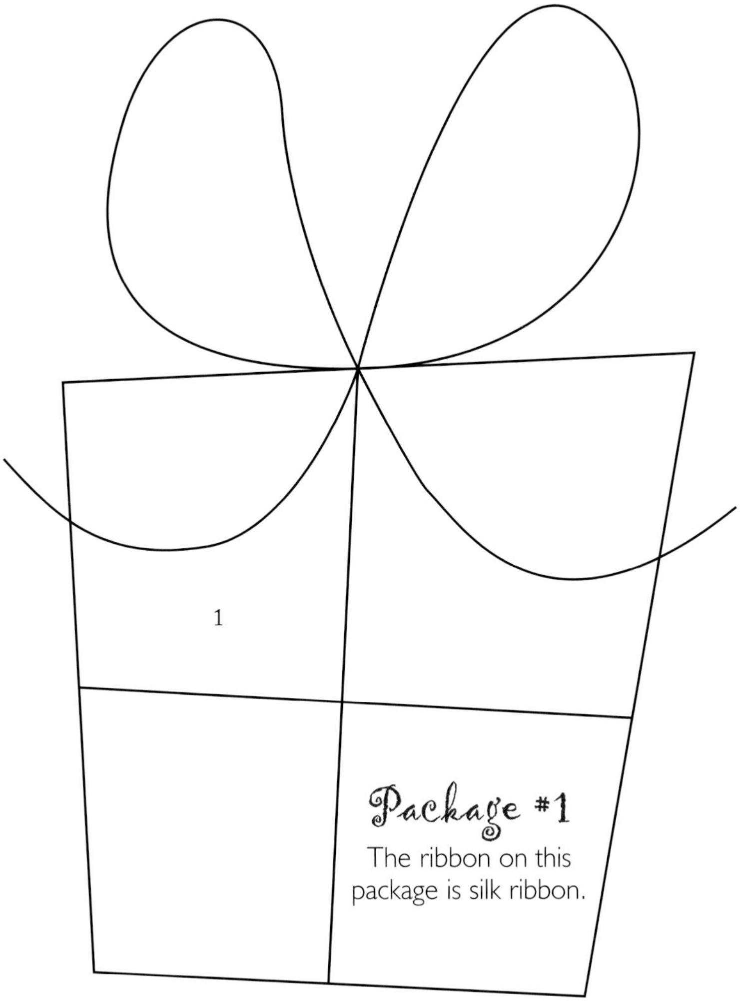

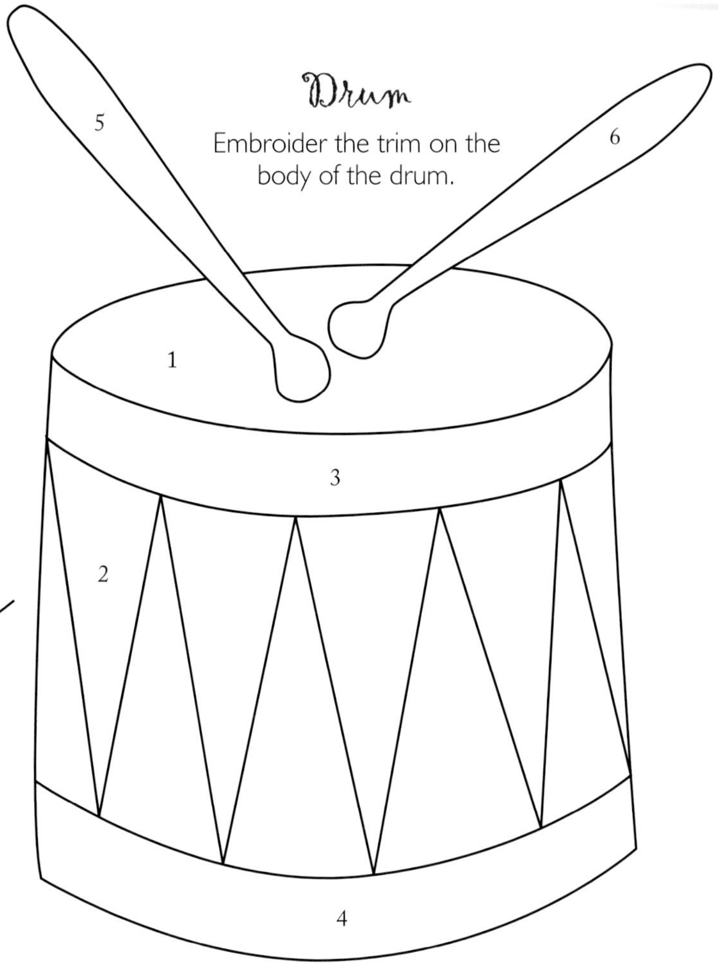

Drum
Embroider the trim on the
body of the drum.

5

6

1

3

2

4

1

Package #1
The ribbon on this
package is silk ribbon.

Blocks
Embroider the letters on the blocks.

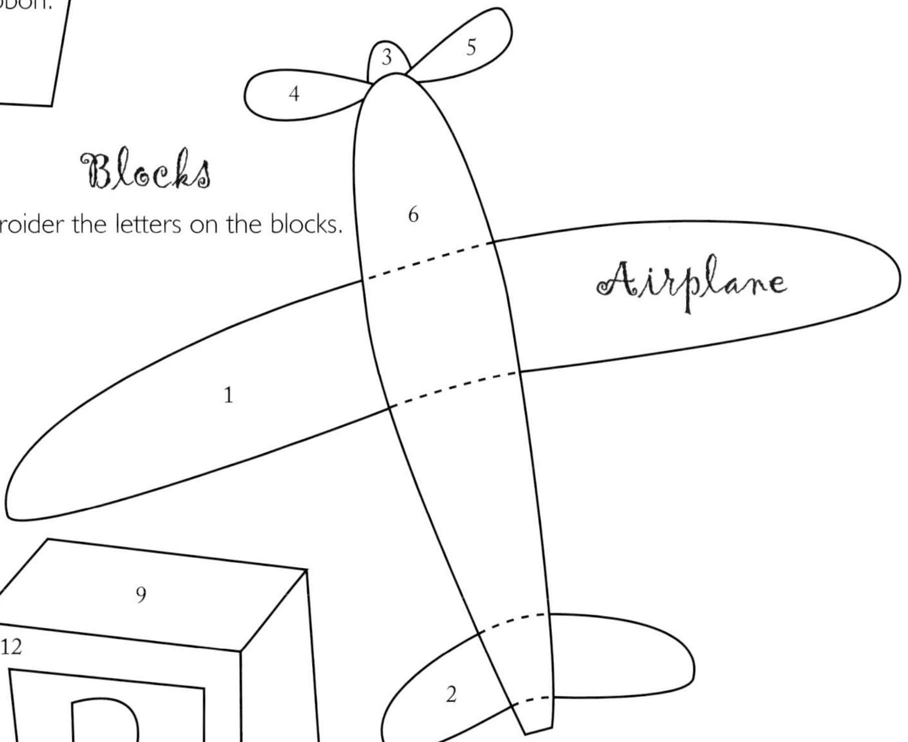

3   5
4

6

1

Airplane

2

6
8
7
A

1
3
B X
2
5
4

9
12
R
11
10
2

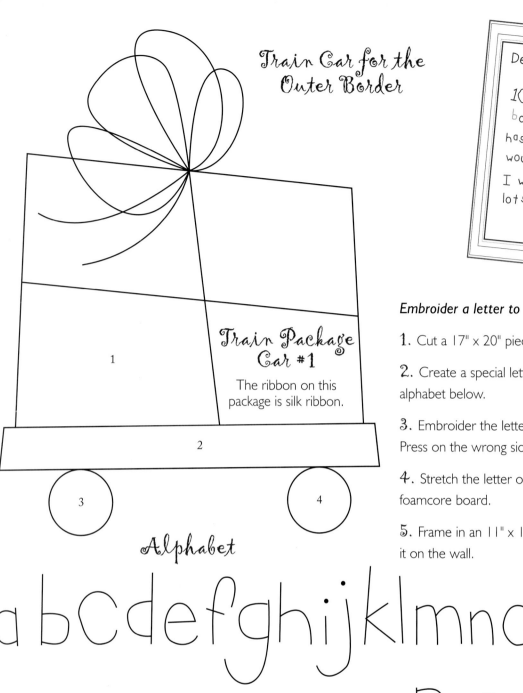

Train Car for the Outer Border

Train Package Car #1

The ribbon on this package is silk ribbon.

1

2

3

4

Alphabet

Dear Santa
 I want a purple
10 speed bike! No
body that I know
has one and that
would be so cool.
I will leave you
lotsa cookies.
 ♡ AsHLEY

Embroider a letter to Santa to frame for your wall.

1. Cut a 17" x 20" piece of background fabric.

2. Create a special letter to Santa using the alphabet below.

3. Embroider the letter with a backstitch. Press on the wrong side.

4. Stretch the letter over a padded foamcore board.

5. Frame in an 11" x 14" frame and hang it on the wall.

a b c d e f g h i j k l m n o p q r s
t u v w x y z A B C D E F
G H I J K L M N O P
Q R S T U V W X Y Z

The Christmas Trees Quilt

Made by Becky Goldsmith, 2000

Finished appliqué block size: 8" x 8"

Finished Ohio Star block size: 8" x 8"

Finished quilt size: 49½" x 49½"

Becky used a variety of background fabrics for added interest, and she separated the beige backgrounds into two groups: lighter and darker. Note that she used a number of red fabrics as well. The subtle plaids and stripes add another interesting touch to this quilt.

MATERIALS

Darker beige backgrounds and inner border:
A variety of fabrics to total ½ yard

Lighter beige backgrounds and outer border:
A variety of fabrics to total 3 yards

Appliqué: A wide variety of fabric scraps

Red star points, block and border corners:
A variety of fabrics to total ⅞ yard

Brown Christmas light cord: ¾ yard

Binding: ¾ yard

Backing and sleeve: 4 yards

Batting: 54" x 54"

Embroidery floss: A variety of colors

⅜" Bias bar

CUTTING

DARKER BEIGE FABRICS

Inner border: Cut 4 strips 1¼" x 40½".

Ohio Star centers: Cut 13 squares 4½" x 4½".

LIGHTER BEIGE FABRICS

Outer border: Cut 4 strips lengthwise 6" x 43½".

Tree block backgrounds: Cut 12 squares 10" x 10".

Star block corners: Cut 52 squares 2½" x 2½".

Star block sides: Cut 52 rectangles 2½" x 4½".

RED FABRICS

Block corners: Cut 48 squares 2½" x 2½".

Ohio Star points: Cut 104 squares 2½" x 2½".

Inner border corners: Cut 4 squares 1¼" x 1¼".

Outer border corners: Cut 4 squares 4½" x 4½".

BROWN FABRIC

Christmas light cord: Cut 1 square 23" x 23" to make 1½"-wide continuous bias. Make the finished bias stem ⅜" wide. (Refer to page 62 for instructions.)

Binding: Cut 1 square 23" x 23" to make 2½"-wide continuous bias binding (refer to pages 59-60 for instructions).

BLOCK ASSEMBLY

Tree Blocks

The blocks are numbered from left to right, top to bottom. For example, Block #1 is located in the upper left hand corner of the quilt. The full-size appliqué patterns are on pages 19–24. Because they are placed to fit on the pages, they are not in numerical order.

1. Appliqué the trees to the 10" squares. Refer to pages 49–55 for instructions on making placement overlays and preparing the appliqué.

▦ Appliqué Tips

Use the *circle appliqué* technique for the tree ornaments and the *cutaway appliqué* technique for the small or irregularly shaped pieces such as the stars, tree trunks, and leaves. (Refer to pages 56-57 for instructions.)

2. Embroider the trees that have embroidery embellishments.

3. After the appliqué and embroidery are complete, press the blocks on the wrong side.

4. Trim the blocks to 8½" x 8½".

5. Either mark the diagonal on the back of the 2½" red squares or refer to Piecing Triangle Corners on page 59 and sew a 2½" red square to each corner of each tree block. Trim excess ¼" away from the seamline. Press open.

Add corner squares and trim excess.

Ohio Star Blocks

▦ Sewing Tip

For a quick way to sew the star points without marking the diagonal lines, refer to Piecing Triangle Corners on page 59 or use the following instructions.

1. Draw a diagonal line on the wrong side of the 2½" x 2½" star points.

2. Place a 2½" x 2½" star point over one half of a 2½" x 4½" rectangle, right sides together. Sew on the drawn line.

3. Trim the excess ¼" away from the seamline, as shown. Press open.

4. Place a 2½" x 2½" star point over the other half of the rectangle, right sides together. Sew on the drawn line.

5. Trim the excess ¼" away from the seamline. Press open.

6. Arrange the pieced units and corner squares. Sew them together into three rows as shown. Sew rows together to finish the star. Press the seams in one direction. This block is now 8½" x 8½".

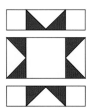

7. Make 12 more Ohio Stars.

BORDER ASSEMBLY

Border Appliqué

1. Copy and tape the border appliqué patterns together and make a placement overlay. The patterns are on pages 25-28.

2. Press each border background in half horizontally and vertically to establish the center lines.

3. Appliqué the borders. Refer to page 62, for instructions on making ⅜" bias stem for the Christmas light cord.

4. After the appliqué is complete, press the borders on the wrong side.

5. Trim the borders to 4½" x 42".

QUILT ASSEMBLY

When sewing the borders, press the seam allowances toward the border after each step.

1. Sew the blocks together into rows. Press the seams in each row in an alternate direction so the seams nest when the rows are sewn together.

2. Sew the rows together. Press the seams in one direction.

3. Sew the side inner borders to the quilt.

4. Sew a small red square to each end of the top and bottom inner borders. Press.

5. Sew the top and bottom inner border strips to the quilt.

6. Sew the side outer borders to the quilt.

7. Sew a large red square to each end of the top and bottom outer borders. Press.

8. Sew the top and bottom outer borders to the quilt.

9. Finish the quilt. Refer to pages 55, 59–61 for instructions.

Quilt Assembly Diagram

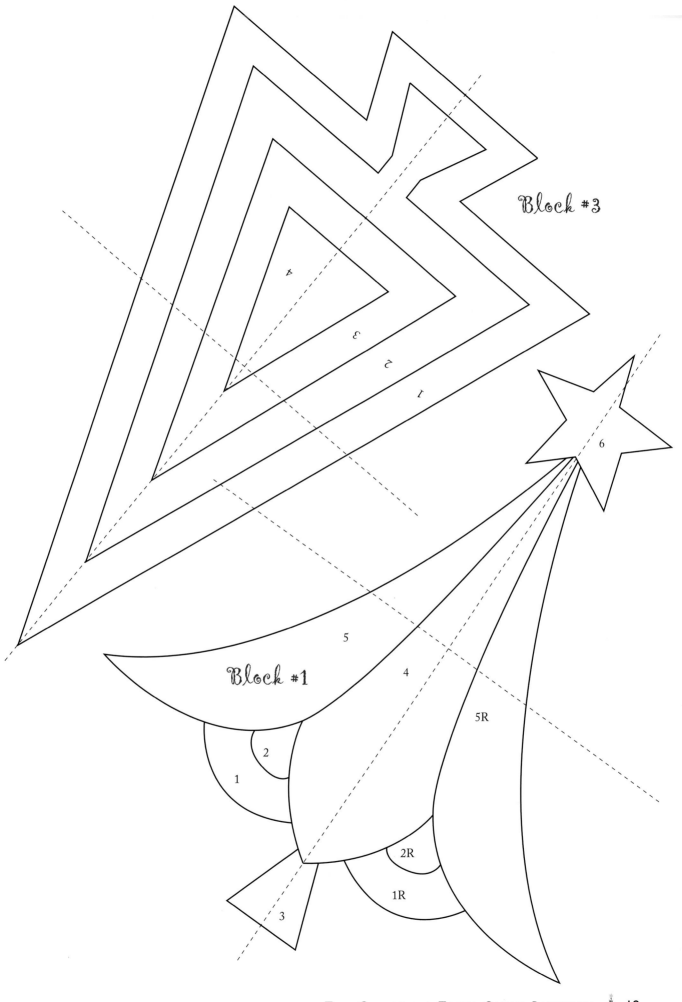

Block #3

Block #1

Block #5

Block #2

Embroider a swag on the dashed line.

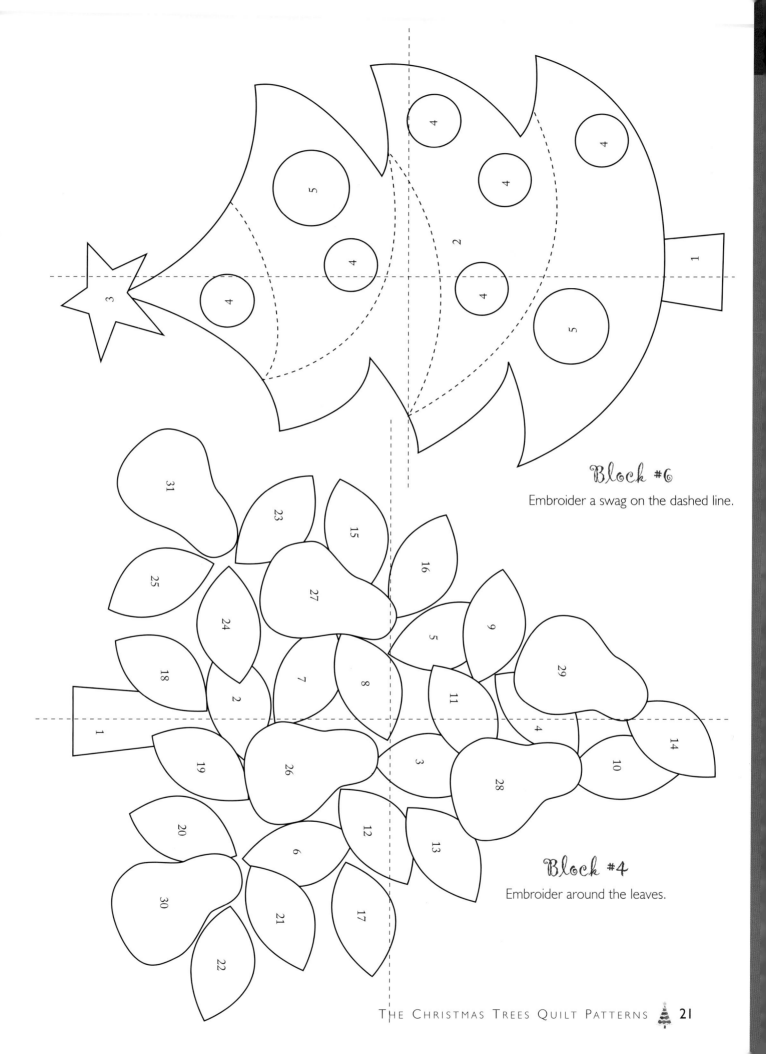

Block #6
Embroider a swag on the dashed line.

Block #4
Embroider around the leaves.

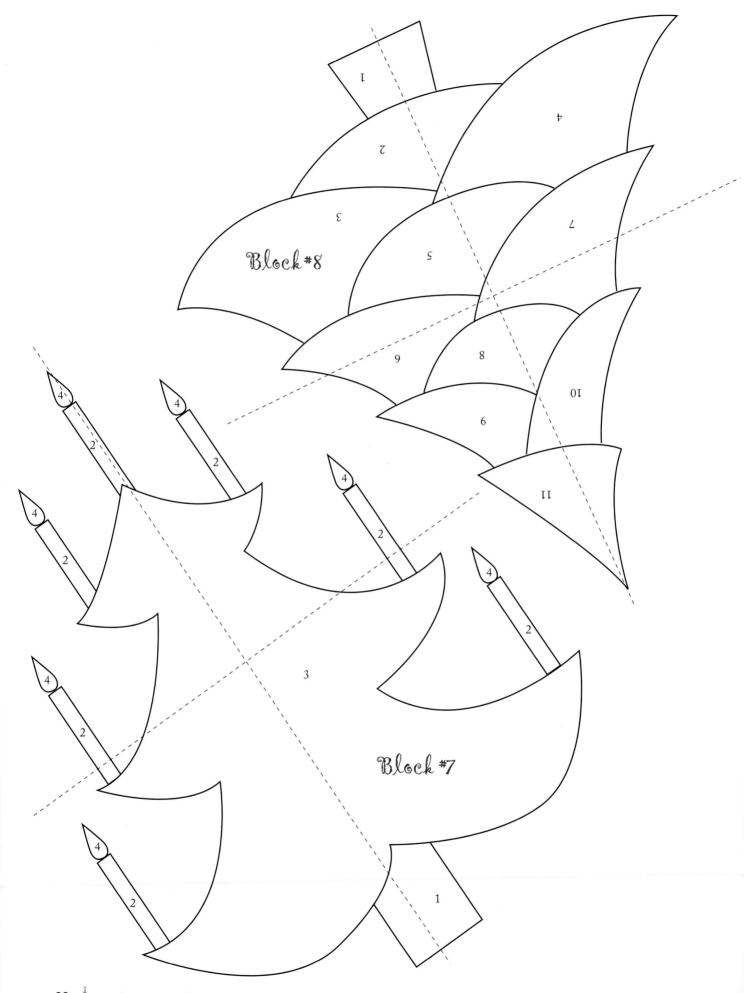

Block #8

Block #7

Block #10

Embroider on the dashed lines.

Block #9

23

Block #11

Embroider on the dashed lines.

3

1

2

6

4

3

2

1

5

8

7

Block #12

Embroider on the dashed lines.

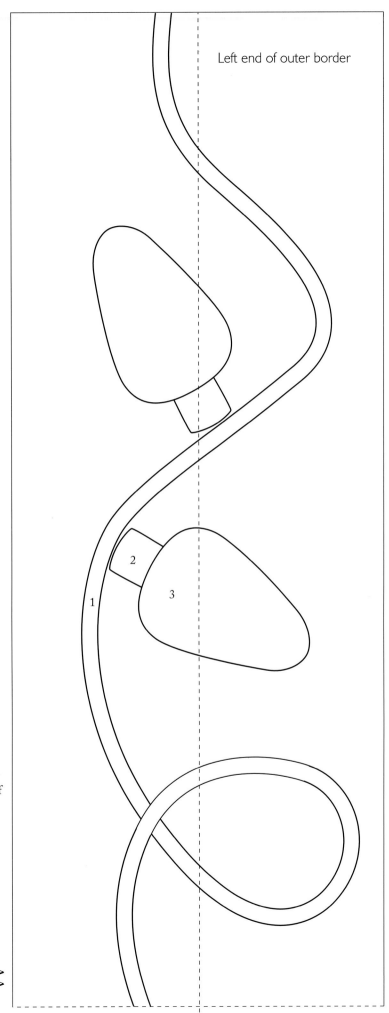

Left end of outer border

1

2

3

Match the letters at the edges of the four outer border sections found on the following pages.

AA

AA

BB

Center

BB

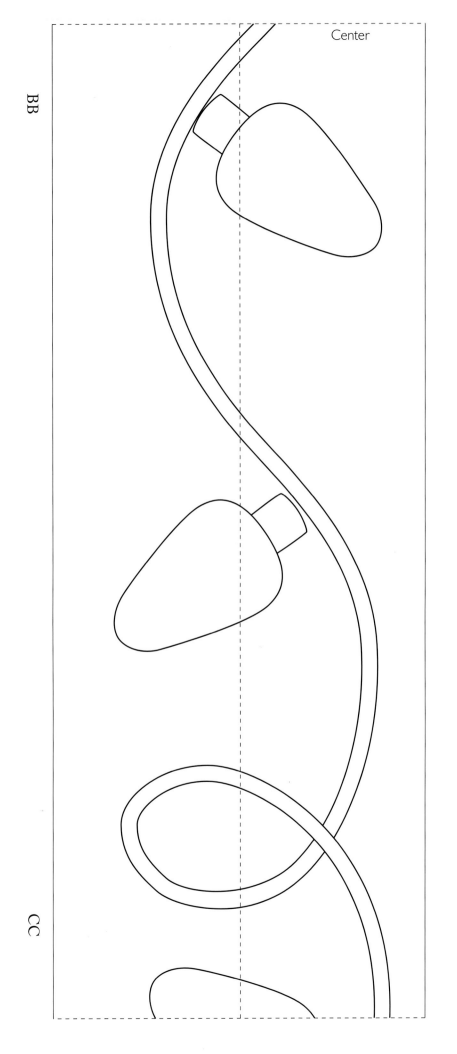

CC

CC

Right end of outer border

Poinsettia Quilt

Photo by Sharon Risedorph

**Made by Linda Jenkins & Becky Goldsmith,
Quilted by Linda Jenkins, 2002**

Finished appliqué block size: 10" x 10"

Finished quilt size: 27" x 27"

Warm rosy-pink poinsettias glow on a chocolate brown background in this elegant little quilt. You'll enjoy these poinsettias even more than the real thing!

MATERIALS

Brown backgrounds: A variety of fabrics to total ¾ yard

Appliqué: A wide variety of fabric scraps

Pink plaid sashing: ⅓ yard

Red border: ⅓ yard

Striped binding: ⅔ yard

Back and sleeve: 1 yard

Batting: 31" x 31"

Green embroidery floss

CUTTING

BROWN FABRICS

Background: Cut 16 squares 6½" x 6½".

PINK PLAID FABRIC

Sashing: Cut 5 strips 1½" x width of the fabric and cut into:

  A. 2 strips 1½" x 10½" for short sashing between blocks.

  B. 3 strips 1½" x 21½" for sashing between rows.

  C. 2 strips 1½" x 23½" for side sashing.

RED FABRIC

Border: Cut 4 strips 2½" x width of the fabric and cut into:

  2 strips 2½" x 23½" for top and bottom borders.

  2 strips 2½" x 27½" for side borders.

STRIPED FABRIC

Binding: Cut 1 square 20" x 20" to make 2½"-wide continuous bias binding (refer to pages 59-60 for instructions).

BLOCK ASSEMBLY

The full-size appliqué patterns are on pages 32–33. Note that the upper right and lower left blocks are mirror images of the pattern. (Refer to photograph on page 29.)

1. Sew four 6½" squares together for the block background. Make four.

2. Appliqué the blocks. Refer to pages 49–55 for instructions on making placement overlays and preparing the appliqué.

🔲 *Appliqué Tips*

Use the *cutaway appliqué* technique for the branches and the *circle appliqué* technique for the berries. (Refer to pages 56 and 57 for instructions.)

3. Embroider French knots in the center of each poinsettia.

4. After the appliqué is complete, press the blocks on the wrong side.

5. Trim the blocks to 10½" x 10½".

QUILT ASSEMBLY

When sewing the sashings, press the seam allowances toward the sashing after each step. When sewing the borders, press the seam allowances toward the border after each step.

1. Sew the blocks and short sashings (A) together into rows.

2. Sew the rows together with the horizontal sashing strips (B).

3. Sew the side sashings (C) to the quilt.

4. Sew the side outer borders to the quilt.

5. Sew the top and bottom outer borders to the quilt.

6. Finish the quilt. Refer to pages 55, 59–61 for instructions.

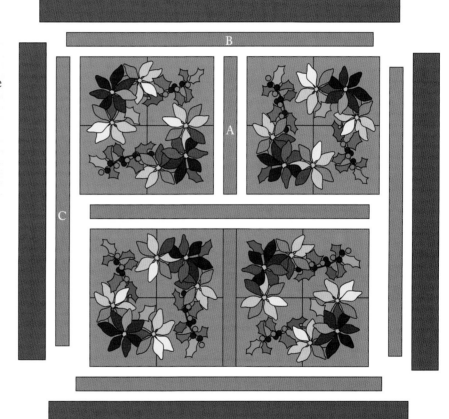

Quilt Assembly Diagram

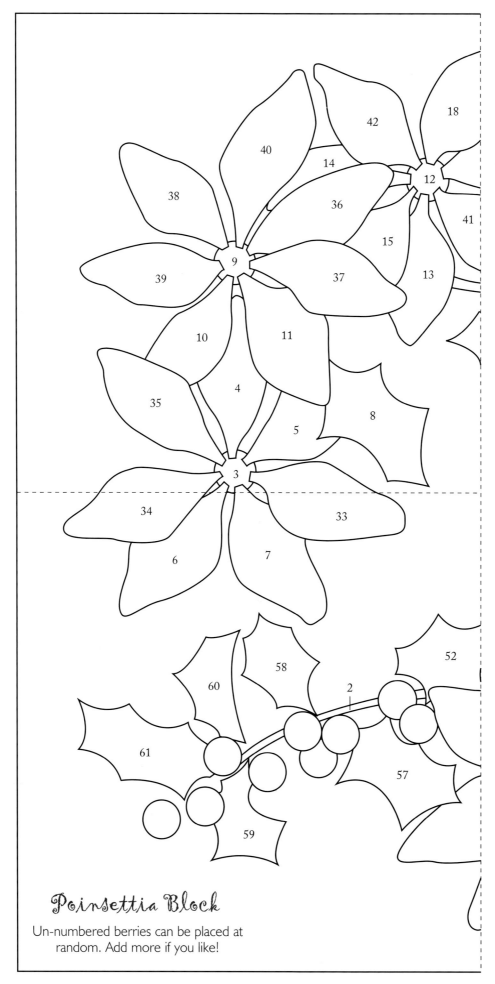

Poinsettia Block

Un-numbered berries can be placed at random. Add more if you like!

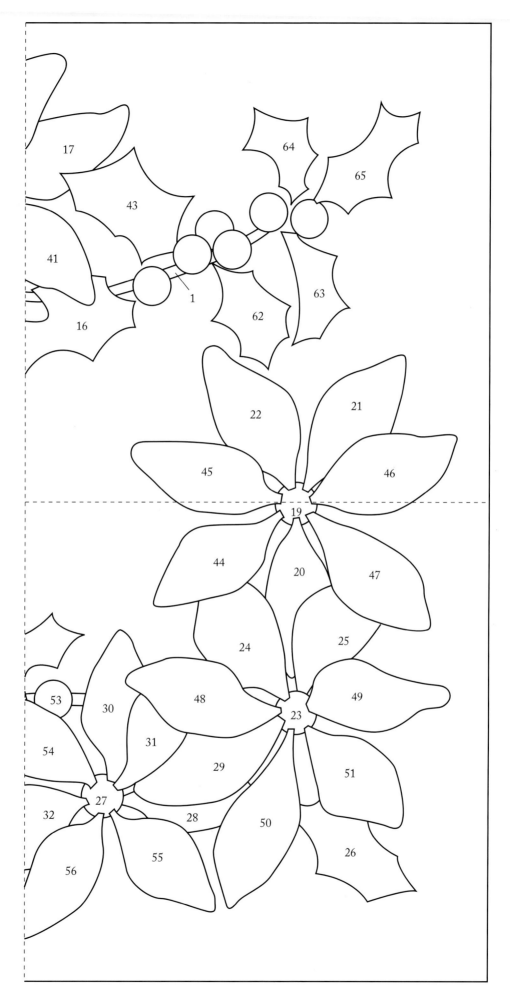

A Sampling of Santas Quilt

Made by Becky Goldsmith, 1994

Finished appliqué block sizes: 10" x 10" and 10" x 21½"

Finished quilt size: 56" x 67½"

The Christmas season is a time of joy and sharing with family and friends. We are particularly fond of Santa as a symbol of this season and a reminder of happy times—past, present, and future.

General Appliqué Instructions

We have a great way to do appliqué using sturdy laminated appliqué templates and a clear vinyl positioning overlay that makes it a snap to position all the pieces. If you're new to Piece O' Cake Designs appliqué techniques, read through the General Appliqué Instructions before beginning a project.

For a complete guide to hand appliqué, refer to our book *The Appliqué Sampler.*

PREPARING THE BACKGROUNDS FOR APPLIQUÉ

Always cut the background fabric larger than the size it will be when it is pieced into the quilt. The outer edges of the block can stretch and fray when you handle it while stitching. The appliqué can shift during stitching and cause the block to shrink slightly. For these reasons it is best to add 1" to all sides of the backgrounds when you cut them out. You will trim the blocks to size after the appliqué is complete.

1. Press each background block in half vertically and horizontally. This establishes a center grid in the background that will line up with the center grid on the positioning overlay.

Press to create a centering grid.

MAKING THE APPLIQUÉ TEMPLATES

Each appliqué shape requires a template and we have a unique way to make templates that is both easy and accurate.

1. Use a photocopier to make 2-5 copies of each block. Compare your copies with the original to be sure they are accurate.

2. Cut out each shape that you need a template for from these copies. Leave a little paper allowance around each shape. Where one shape overlaps another, cut the top shape from one copy and the bottom shape from another copy. In cases where shapes don't overlap, you may be able to cut out groups of shapes from the paper, then cut individual shapes after placing them on the laminate.

Cut out appliqué shapes.

3. Take a self-laminating sheet and place it shiny side down on the table in front of you. Peel the paper backing off, leaving the sticky side up.

4. If you are doing hand appliqué, place the templates drawn side down. For fusible appliqué, place the blank side down. Take care when placing each template onto the laminate. Use more laminating sheets as necessary.

Place appliqué shapes drawn side down on self-laminating sheets for hand appliqué.

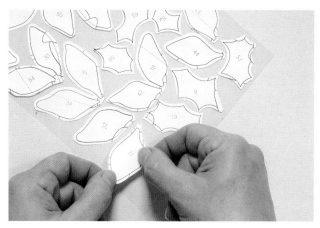

Place appliqué shapes blank side down on self-laminating sheets for fusible appliqué.

5. Cut out each individual shape. Try to split the drawn line—don't cut inside or outside of the line. Keep edges smooth and points sharp.

Cut out each template.

You'll notice how easy these templates are to cut out. That's the main reason we like this method. It is also true that a mechanical copy of the pattern is more accurate than hand tracing onto template plastic. As you use the templates you will see that they are sturdy and hold up to repeated use.

USING THE TEMPLATES FOR HAND APPLIQUÉ

For needle-turn (hand) appliqué, the templates are used right side up on the right side of the fabric.

1. Place the appliqué fabric right side up on a sandpaper board.

2. Place the template right side up (shiny side up) on the fabric so that as many edges as possible are on the diagonal grain of the fabric. A bias edge is easier to turn under than one that is on the straight of grain.

3. Trace around the template. The sandpaper will hold the fabric in place while you trace.

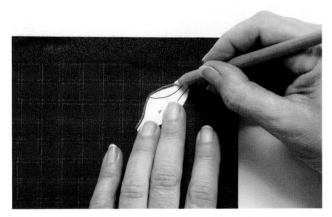

Place templates with as many edges as possible on the bias and trace around each template.

4. Cut out each piece, adding a ³⁄₁₆" turn-under allowance.

Cut out each piece adding ³⁄₁₆" turn-under allowance.

5. Before placing appliqué pieces on the block, finger-press the turn-under allowances. This is a very important step. As you finger-press, make sure that the drawn line is pressed to the back. You'll be amazed at how much easier this one step makes needleturning the turn-under allowance.

Finger-press each piece with the drawn line to the back.

6. Prepare all the appliqué pieces for a block and follow the instructions on pages 52-55 to make and use the positioning overlay.

USING THE TEMPLATES FOR FUSIBLE APPLIQUÉ

For fusible appliqué, templates are used with the drawn side down on the wrong side of the fabric. Use a non-stick pressing cloth to protect your iron and ironing board.

1. Follow the instructions for the fusible web you are using and iron it to the **wrong** side of the appliqué fabric. Do not peel off the paper backing.

Iron fusible web to the wrong side of fabric.

2. Leave the fabric right side down. Place the template drawn side down (shiny laminate side up) and trace around it onto the paper backing of the fusible web.

Trace around template onto paper backing.

3. Cut out the appliqué pieces on the drawn line.

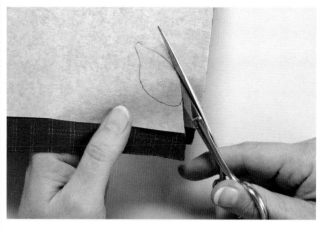

Cut out appliqué pieces on drawn line.

4. Prepare all the appliqué pieces for a block and follow the instructions below to make and use the positioning overlay.

MAKING THE POSITIONING OVERLAY

The positioning overlay is a piece of clear upholstery vinyl that is used to position each appliqué piece accurately on the block. It is easy to make and use, and it makes your projects portable.

1. Cut a piece of clear upholstery vinyl, with its tissue paper lining, to the finished size of each block. Set the tissue paper aside until you are ready to fold or store your overlay.

2. Make a copy of the patterns in this book to work from. Tape pattern pieces together as needed.

3. Tape a copy of a pattern onto the table in front of you.

4. Tape the upholstery vinyl over the pattern. Use a ruler and an ultra fine point Sharpie marker to draw the pattern's horizontal and vertical center lines onto the vinyl.

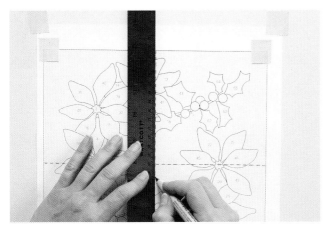

Trace vinyl over pattern and draw center lines.

5. Trace all the lines from the pattern accurately onto the vinyl. The numbers on the pattern indicate stitching sequence—include these numbers on the overlay.

Trace pattern onto the vinyl.

USING THE POSITIONING OVERLAY FOR HAND APPLIQUÉ

1. Place the background right side up on the work surface.

2. Place the overlay right side up on top of the background.

3. Line up the center grid of the fabric with the center grid of the overlay.

Place overlay on background and line up grids.

4. Pin the overlay if necessary to keep it from shifting out of position.

5. Finger-press appliqué piece #1 and place it under the overlay but on top of the background. It is easy to tell when the appliqué pieces are in position under the overlay. As you work, finger-press and position one piece at a time. Be sure to follow the appliqué order.

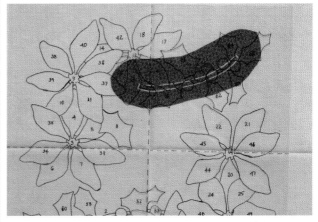

Use overlay to position appliqué pieces. (Note: This piece has been cut to use the cutaway appliqué technique, refer to page 56.)

6. Fold the overlay back and pin the appliqué piece in place using ½" sequin pins. We generally position and stitch only one or two pieces at a time. Remove the vinyl overlay before stitching.

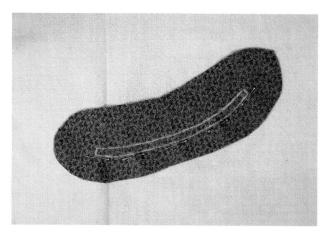

Pin appliqué piece in place.

7. Hand appliqué the piece in place with an invisible stitch and matching thread.

8. When you are ready to put away the overlay, place the tissue paper over the drawn side before you fold it. The tissue paper keeps the lines from transferring from one part of the vinyl to another.

USING THE POSITIONING OVERLAY FOR FUSIBLE APPLIQUÉ

1. Place the background right side up on an ironing board.

2. Place the overlay right side up on top of the back-ground.

3. Line up the center grid of the fabric with the center grid of the overlay.

Place overlay on background and line up grids.

4. Peel off the paper backing from each appliqué piece.

5. Place the appliqué pieces right side up, under the overlay but on top of the background. Start with the #1 appliqué piece and follow the appliqué order. It is easy to tell when the appliqué pieces are in position under the overlay. Often you can position many pieces at once.

Use overlay to position appliqué pieces.

6. Carefully remove the overlay and iron the appliqué pieces in place. Be sure to follow the instructions for your brand of fusible web. Do not touch the overlay vinyl with the iron because it will melt.

Fuse appliqué pieces in place.

7. After fusing cotton fabric, we sew the raw edges of the fused appliqué with a straight or blanket stitch and matching thread on the sewing machine. As the quilts are used, the machine stitching keeps the edges secure.

PRESSING AND TRIMMING THE BLOCKS

1. Press the blocks on the wrong side after the appliqué is complete. If the ironing surface is hard, place the blocks on a towel and the appliqué will not get flattened.

2. Carefully trim each block to size. Always make sure the design is properly aligned with the ruler before you cut off the excess fabric.

FINISHING THE QUILT

1. Assemble your quilt top following the instructions for each project.

2. Construct the back of the quilt, piecing as needed.

3. Place the backing right side down on a firm surface. Tape it down to keep it from moving around while you are basting.

4. Place your batting over the backing and pat out any wrinkles.

5. Center the quilt top right side up over the batting.

6. Baste the layers together.

7. Quilt the quilt by hand or machine.

8. Trim the outer edges and finish the outer edge with continuous bias binding (refer to page 59). Sew on any hard embellishments (buttons, beads, etc.) now.

MAKING A LABEL AND SLEEVE

1. Make and attach a hanging sleeve to the back of the quilt.

2. Make a label and sew it to the back of the quilt. Include information that you want people to know about your quilt. Your name and address, the date, the fiber content of the quilt and batting, if it was made for a special person or occasion—these are all things that can go on the label.

Special Techniques

CUTAWAY APPLIQUÉ

The cutaway technique makes it much easier to stitch very small pieces or irregular, long, thin pieces such as stems.

1. Place the template on top of the selected fabric. Be sure to place the template on the fabric so that most of the edges will be on the diagonal grain of the fabric. Trace around the template.

2. Cut out the appliqué piece leaving 1" or more of excess fabric around the traced shape. Be sure to leave fabric intact between star points, the "V" between branches, and so on.

3. Finger-press, making sure the drawn line is pressed to the back.

4. Use the vinyl overlay to position the appliqué piece. Pin it in place, positioning the pins ¼" away from the edge that will be stitched first. When a shape is curved, always sew the concave side first if possible.

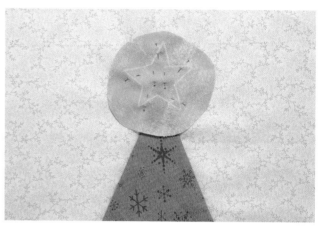

5. Begin cutting the excess fabric away from where you will start stitching, leaving a ³⁄₁₆" or smaller turn-under allowance. Start stitching on a straight edge, not a corner or point.

6. Trim away more fabric as you sew. Clip inner points as needed.

7. Remove the pins as you stitch the next side of the piece. Clip away excess fabric as necessary.

8. Continue until all sides of the appliqué piece are stitched.

CIRCLE APPLIQUÉ

If you have never needle-turn appliquéd a circle, try our method. You'll get a nice circle every time.

1. Trace circles onto selected fabric. Cut out each circle, adding a ³⁄₁₆" turn-under allowance.

2. Finger-press the turn-under allowance making sure the drawn line is pressed to the back.

3. Use the vinyl overlay to position the appliqué piece onto the block. Pin it in place. Use at least 2 pins to keep the circle from shifting.

4. Begin sewing. Turn under only enough turn-under allowance to take 1 or 2 stitches. You can only control 1 stitch at a time.

5. Use the tip of your needle to reach under the appliqué and open up any folds and to smooth out any points.

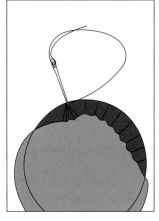

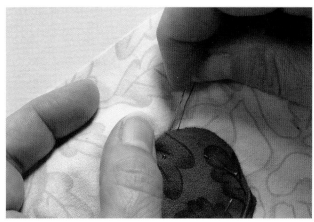

6. For the last few stitches, as you fold and turn under the remaining turn-under allowance the circle will tend to flatten out.

7. Use the tip of your needle to smooth out any pleats in the turn-under allowance and to pull the flattened part of the circle into a more rounded shape.

REVERSE APPLIQUÉ

Use reverse appliqué when you want to cut through one piece of fabric to reveal the fabric below it.

1. Place the template with the opening in it on top of the selected fabric. Be sure to place the template on the fabric so that most of the edges will be on the diagonal grain of the fabric. Trace around the template.

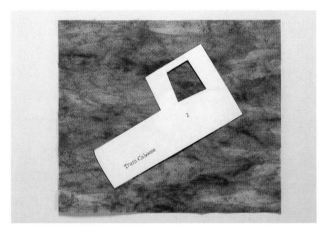

2. Cut out the appliqué piece. Leave 1" or more of excess fabric around it. Don't cut out the opening yet, but finger-press it, making sure the drawn line is pressed to the back.

3. Position the appliqué piece on top of the fabric that will show through. Make sure that you leave the bottom fabric large enough so you can handle it easily. Pin the appliqué piece in place. Position the pins ¼" away from the edge that will be stitched first.

4. Cut inside the drawn line around the opening leaving a ³⁄₁₆" turn-under allowance. Begin sewing and clip corners as needed. Never begin sewing at a point or corner.

5. Finish sewing the opening. Turn the unit over and cut away the excess bottom fabric, leaving a ³⁄₁₆" seam allowance.

PIECING TRIANGLE CORNERS

Here's a neat trick for sewing the diagonal line on triangle corners without marking.

1. Put a piece of paper or ruler squarely on the bed of the sewing machine. Line up one side of the paper or ruler with the spot where the needle makes the stitch.

2. Stick a 3"–4" length of blue painter's tape in front of the throat plate in line with the edge of the paper or ruler. The edge of the paper or ruler will be aligned with the stitching path. The painter's tape is easy to see and easy to remove.

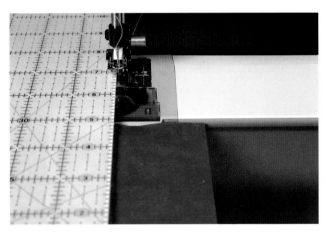

3. Align the diagonal corners with the needle and the edge of the tape.

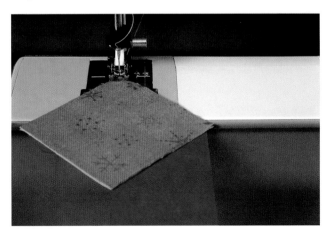

4. Sew from corner to corner.

MAKING CONTINUOUS BIAS

The vine-like cord for the Christmas tree lights on the borders of The Christmas Trees quilt is easy if you make a continuous bias stem. Continuous bias binding is also a lovely edge for any quilt. It's worth the effort to learn this easy technique so your bindings complement your quilt. We show you how to master those tricky binding corners on pages 60–61.

1. Start with a square of fabric and cut it in half diagonally.

2. Sew the two triangles together, right sides together, as shown. Be sure to sew the edges that are on the straight of grain.

3. If you are using striped fabric, be sure to match the stripes. You may need to offset the fabric a little to make the stripes match.

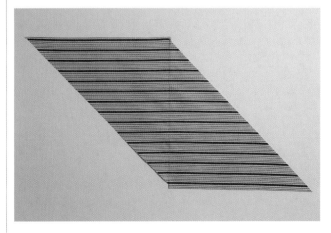

4. For bias for stems, press the seams to one side; otherwise press the seam allowances open. Cut the desired width into each side about 4" as shown.

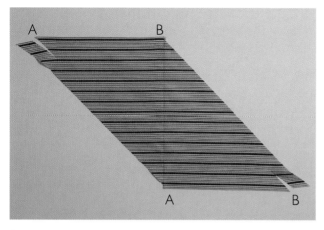

5. Match the A's and B's with the fabric right sides together. Sew and press the seam.

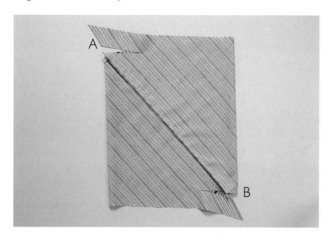

6. Use a rotary cutter and ruler to cut the continuous bias strip at the desired width. Rotate fabric as necessary.

⚏ *Cutting Tip for Continuous Bias*

Try putting a small cutting mat on the end of your ironing board. Slide the tube of fabric over it. Use a ruler and rotary cutter to cut the long strip of continuous bias, rotating the tube of fabric as needed.

Cut using gentle pressure—if your ironing board is padded, the cutting surface may give if you press very hard.

SEWING BINDING TO THE QUILT

1. Cut the first end of the binding at a 45° angle. Turn this end under ¼" and press.

2. Press the continuous binding strip in half lengthwise, wrong sides together.

3. With raw edges even, pin the binding to the edge of the quilt beginning a few inches away from a corner. Start sewing 6" from the beginning of the binding strip using a ¼" seam allowance.

4. Stop ¼" away from the corner and backstitch several stitches.

5. Fold the binding straight up as shown. Note the 45° angle.

6. Fold the binding straight down and begin sewing the next side of the quilt.

7. Sew the binding to all sides of the quilt, following the process above for the corners. Stop a few inches before you reach the beginning of the binding, but don't trim the excess binding yet.

8. Overlap the ends of the binding and cut the second end at a 90° angle. **Be sure to cut the binding long enough so the cut end is covered completely by the angled end.**

9. Slip the end that is cut at 90° into the angled end.

10. Pin the joined ends to the quilt and finish sewing the binding to the quilt.

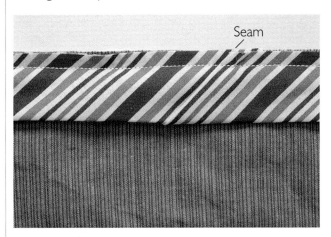

Seam

11. Turn the binding to the back of the quilt, covering the raw edges. Stitch the folded edge of the binding by hand to the back of the quilt.

MAKING BIAS STEMS

1. Make a continuous bias strip 1 ½" wide (refer to pages 59-60 for instructions). Press the strip in half lengthwise with the wrong sides together.

2. Place the folded edge of the bias strip along the ⅜" line on the seam guide of your sewing machine. Sew the length of the bias strip.

3. Trim away the excess fabric, leaving a very scant seam allowance.

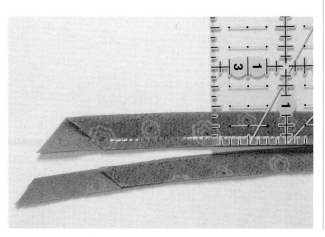

4. Insert the ⅜" bias bar into the sewn bias tube. Shift the seam to the back of the bar and press it in place. Remove the bias bar.

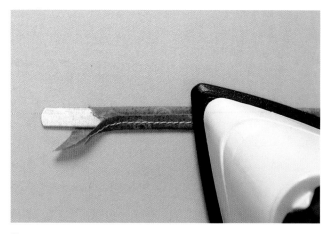

5. Hold up the finished bias stem. Notice that it curves more in one direction than the other. The side closest to the seam line makes the tighter curve. When possible, match this side of the bias stem to the concave side of the stem on your pattern.

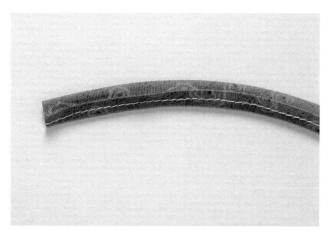

6. This technique can be used for any width bias stem.

OTHER FAVORITES BY PIECE O' CAKE DESIGNS

The Appliqué Sampler
Learn to Appliqué the
Piece O' Cake Way!

Once Upon a Season
Nine Appliquéd and Pieced Quilts,
Celebrating Every Season

Dear Pin Pal!
25 Pin Pal Blocks & Quilts
from Becky & Linda

**Contemporary Classics
in Plaids & Stripes**
9 Projects from Piece O' Cake Designs

BLOCKS OF THE MONTH

Tulips in the Park

Cinnamon Stitches

Simply Delicious!

Thru Grandmother's Window

Land of the Free

Flourishes

**A Walk in the
Mountains**

About the Authors

Linda Jenkins and Becky Goldsmith

The Green Country Quilter's Guild in Tulsa, Oklahoma can be credited for bringing together Linda Jenkins and Becky Goldsmith. Their friendship developed while they worked together on many guild projects and through a shared love for appliqué. This partnership led to the birth of Piece O' Cake Designs in 1994, and survived Linda's move to Pagosa Springs, Colorado while Becky headed for Sherman, Texas.

Linda owned and managed a beauty salon before she started quilting. Over the years she developed a fine eye for color as a hair colorist and makeup artist. Becky's degree in interior design and many art classes provided a perfect background for quilting. Linda and Becky have shown many quilts and have won numerous awards. Together they make a dynamic quilting duo, and love to teach other quilters the joys of appliqué.

In the fall of 2002 Becky and Linda joined the C&T Publishing family where they continue to produce wonderful books and patterns.

Other Fine Books From C&T

FOR MORE INFORMATION
WRITE FOR A FREE CATALOG:
C&T Publishing, Inc., P.O. Box 1456,
Lafayette, CA 94549
(800) 284-1114
e-mail: ctinfo@ctpub.com
website: www.ctpub.com

QUILTING SUPPLIES
Cotton Patch Mail Order, 3405 Hall Lane,
dept. CTB, Layayette, CA 94549
(800)-835-4418 ▪ (925)-283-7883
website: www.quiltusa.com
email: quiltusa@yahoo.com

Note: Fabrics used in the quilts shown may not be currently available since fabric manufacturers keep most fabrics in print for only a short time.

Index